Table of Contents

Who Am I?

I'm white and
furry, and I
swim in the sea.

The cold snow
and ice are just
right for me.

Who am I?
A polar bear!

Big Bears!

Have you seen a polar bear in a zoo?
Polar bears are big—really big.

They are the biggest meat-eaters
on land. A polar bear can weigh as
much as seven men!

A polar bear's body is built for the Arctic. These bears have thick fur to keep them warm.

Polar bears have thick fat, too. The fat keeps body heat in and keeps the Arctic cold out.

Q How do polar bears stay cool?

A They turn on bear conditioning!

Word Bite

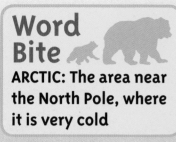

ARCTIC: The area near the North Pole, where it is very cold

9

Powerful Paws

Long, thick, curved claws grab food easily.

Thick pads keep feet warm.

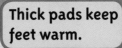

Front paws are webbed, like ducks' feet. This helps polar bears swim.

Bumps on the footpads keep bears from slipping on the ice.

A polar bear's paws do many things. Paws dig dens in the snow. They break the ice to find food. They also pull food out of the water.

Big paws keep bears from sinking into the snow. The paws are larger than a dinner plate!

Word Bite

DEN: A hidden hole where a wild animal lives. Polar bear mothers have their babies in a den.

Super Swimmers

Polar bears are great swimmers. They spend a lot of time in the water.

Their front paws paddle.
Their back legs steer. Their fat
helps polar bears float.

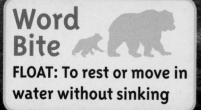

Word Bite

FLOAT: To rest or move in water without sinking

What's for Dinner?

A polar bear eats other animals. Seals are its favorite food. This bear is hunting seals on the sea ice.

Seals come up for air at holes in the ice. The bear waits and waits. Finally, a seal appears. The polar bear snatches it in a flash.

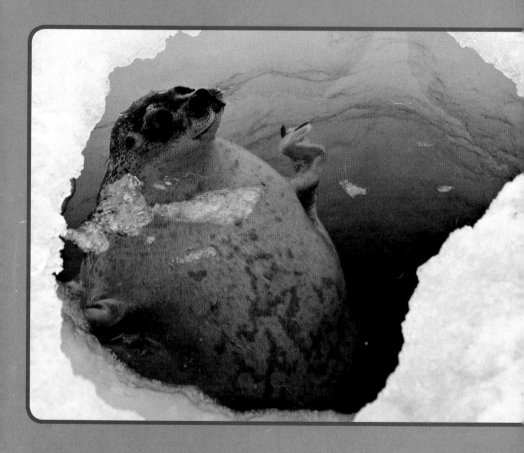

Polar bears have good noses. They can smell a seal 20 miles away!

Polar bears have good hearing and
eyesight, too. These come in handy
when looking for dinner. This bear
has spotted an arctic fox.

The ice melts in spring and summer. Polar bears stay with the ice when they can. They move to land when the sea ice is mostly gone.

On land they usually don't eat at all. Some bears may eat bird eggs. They may eat plants or berries. But there is not much food for polar bears on land.

Q Where do polar bears keep their money?

A In snow banks.

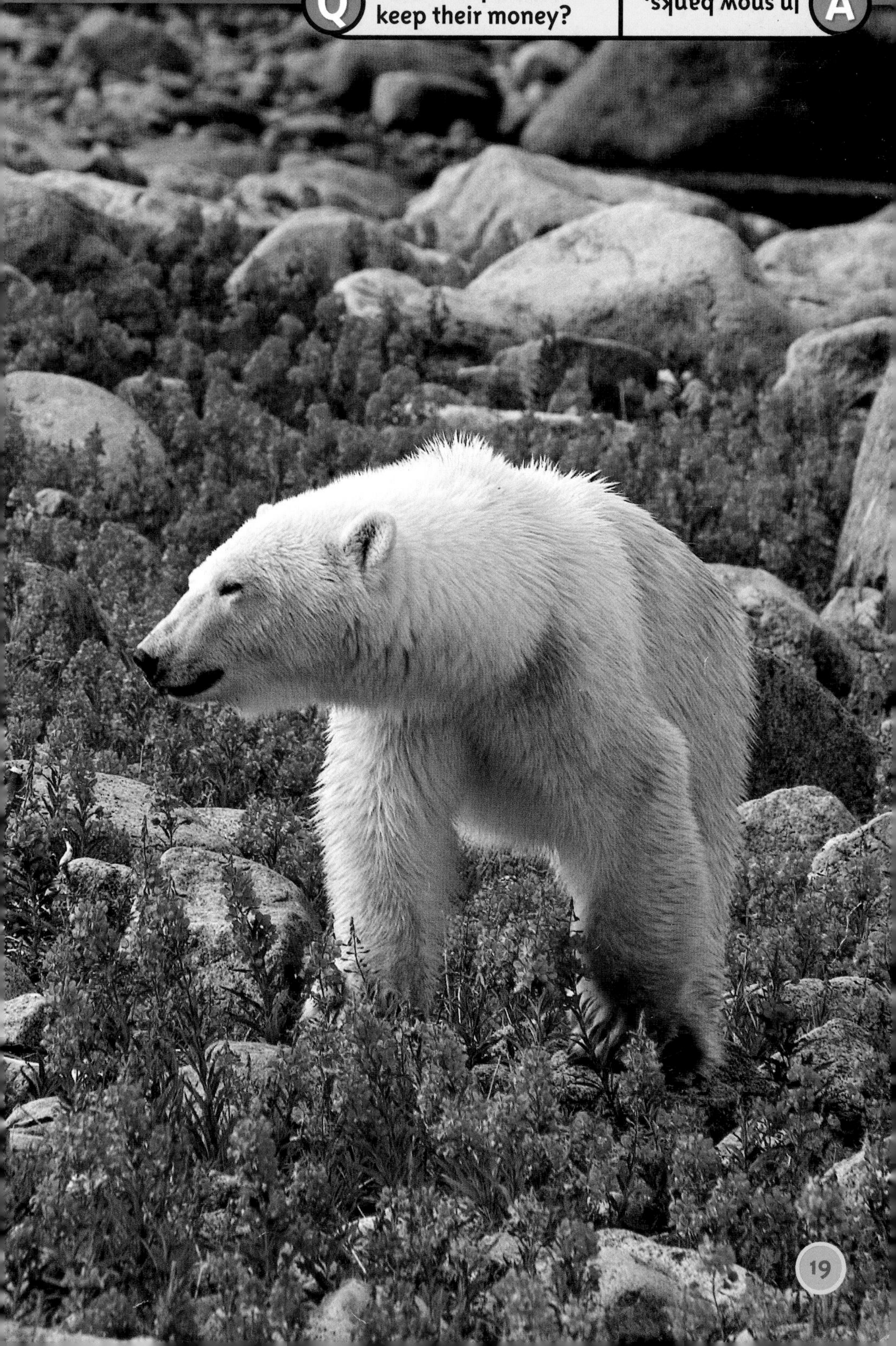

Bears in Town

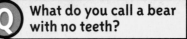

In Churchill, Canada, polar bears come to town in the fall! The ice is melting earlier each year. It is forming later, too. The bears are hungry. They are looking for food.

Our Earth is getting warmer. There is less sea ice now. This is dangerous for polar bears. They need the ice to hunt.

7 Amazing Polar Bear Facts

1

The largest polar bear ever recorded was 2,209 pounds. That's the weight of a small sports car!

2

Polar bears have black skin underneath their white fur.

3

Sometimes polar bears get too hot. Then they take a swim or roll in the snow.

4

Walruses are one of the few animals that polar bears are afraid of.

5

Some people go on vacations to see polar bears. They ride in special buggies to stay safe.

6

Polar bears can eat 100 pounds of seal fat at one time. That's about as heavy as 400 hamburgers!

7

Polar bears clean themselves by rubbing their bodies on the snow.

Cute Cubs

Every new polar bear is special.
A mother bear has babies, called
cubs. She digs a den in the snow.
The cubs stay safe and warm in
the den.

Word
Bite
CUB: A baby bear

The cubs drink their mother's rich milk. They grow quickly. Soon they are big enough to leave the den.

A mother polar bear teaches her cubs to hunt. She also teaches them how to stay safe and warm.

The cubs leave their mother when they are two years old. They are ready to live on their own.

27

Polar bears
like to play just
like you!

Bears wrestle
with each other.
They slide
in the snow.
They like to
play games, too.

Sometimes a cub gets a ride from Mom! These bears are off on an Arctic adventure.

29

What in the World?

These pictures show up-close views of things in a polar bear's world. Use the hints to figure out what's in the pictures. Answers are on page 31.

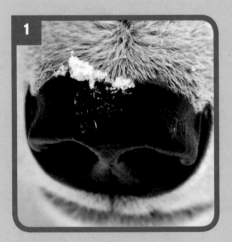

HINT: Helps find dinner

HINT: You don't have one of these.

Walrus	Paw	Tail	Nose	Fur	Seal

3

HINT: A polar bear's favorite food

4

HINT: Keeps a bear warm

5

HINT: Built for snow, ice, and water

6

HINT: Polar bears are afraid of this animal.

ARCTIC: The area near the North Pole, where it is very cold

CUB: A baby bear

DEN: A hidden hole where a wild animal lives. Polar bear mothers have their babies in a den.

FLOAT: To rest or move in water without sinking